and I am the last free bird.

But none could be found…

for a place to rest and breed.

We looked for a place to feed,
for a place to drink,

and spilled and spewed and changed the world.
We could not compete.

and built and paved and dumped

before the people changed the land

and came;

and came,

before people came,

We were suited to our world.
But that was long ago...

and flew in the crisp, clean air.

And there we bred and nested and fed

or in the marshlands.

in the dense forest...

by the sea's edge...

by bubbling brooks...

Once we were many—
living in quiet valleys
and green fields,

For Bill, who knows...

Also by A. Harris Stone
THE CHEMISTRY OF A LEMON
ROCKS AND RILLS: *A Look at Geology* with Dale Ingmanson
TAKE A BALLOON with Bertram Siegel
PLANTS ARE LIKE THAT with Irving Leskowitz

The Last Free Bird by A. Harris Stone and Sheila Heins
©1967 by A. Harris Stone and Sheila Heins
All rights reserved. No part of this book may be
reproduced in any form or by any means, except for
the inclusion of brief quotations in a review, with-
out permission in writing from the publisher.
Library of Congress Catalog Card Number: 67-25420
Printed in the United States of America
J 52399
Prentice-Hall International, Inc., London
Prentice-Hall of Australia, Pty. Ltd., Sydney
Prentice-Hall of Canada, Ltd., Toronto
Prentice-Hall of India Private Ltd., New Delhi
Prentice-Hall of Japan, Inc., Tokyo

Second printing . . . . May, 1971

THE LAST FREE BIRD

by A. Harris Stone
illustrated by Sheila Heins

Prentice-Hall, Inc., Englewood Cliffs, New Jersey

THE LAST FREE BIRD